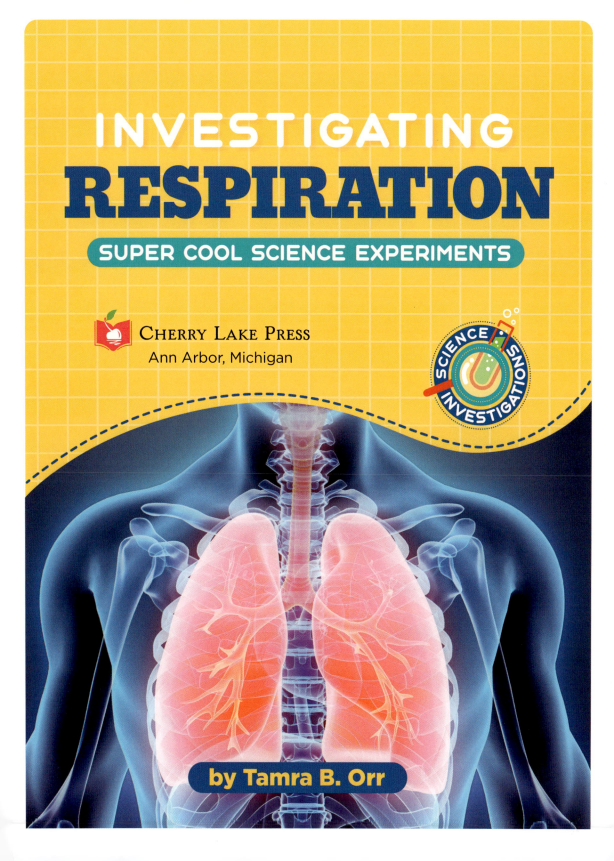

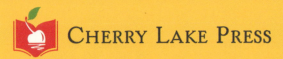# CHERRY LAKE PRESS

Published in the United States of America by
Cherry Lake Publishing Group
Ann Arbor, Michigan
www.cherrylakepublishing.com

Reading Adviser: Beth Walker Gambro, MS, Ed., Reading Consultant, Yorkville, IL

Content Editor: Robert Wolffe, EdD,
Professor of Teacher Education, Bradley University, Peoria, Illinois

Book Designer: Ed Morgan of Bowerbird Books

Photo Credits: cover, title page, © MDGRPHCS/Shutterstock; 4, 9, 10, 11, 13, 14, 17, 18, 21, 22, 25, 26, 28, 29, 30, The Design Lab; 5, © frank60/Shutterstock; 5, 6,7, freepik.com; 8, © GOLFX/Shutterstock; 12, © Olga Guchek/Shutterstock; 15, © HelloRF Zcool/Shutterstock; 19, © Diego Vito Cervo/Dreamstime.com; 24, © Romberi/Shutterstock

Copyright © 2026 by Cherry Lake Publishing

All rights reserved. No part of this book may be reproduced or utilized in any form or by any means without written permission from the publisher.

Cherry Lake Press is an imprint of Cherry Lake Publishing Group.

Library of Congress Cataloging-in-Publication Data has been filed and is available at catalog.loc.gov

Printed in the United States of America

A Note to Parents and Teachers: Please review the instructions for these experiments before your children do them. Be sure to help them with any experiments you do not think they can safely conduct on their own.

A Note to Kids: Be sure to ask an adult for help with these experiments when you need it. Always put your safety first!

Note from Publisher: Websites change regularly, and their future contents are outside of our control. Supervise children when conducting any recommended online searches for extended learning opportunities.

CONTENTS

Breathe Easy! 4

Getting Started 5

Experiment 1: 8
In Through the Nose . . .

Experiment 2: 12
Waste Gas and Cabbage Water

Experiment 3: 16
A Trip Through the Bronchi

Experiment 4: 20
How Much Air?

Experiment 5: 24
It Takes Muscles

Experiment 6: 28
Do It Yourself!

Glossary 30
For More Information 31
Index 32
About the Author 32

Breathe EASY!

In, out, in, out . . . Your body does it all day, every day. It doesn't matter where you are, or if you are awake or asleep. You don't even have to think about it! Can you figure out what it is? Breathing! The complete act of breathing, or **respiration**, is an important body process. The respiratory system is found in your head and chest. This system makes breathing possible.

If you've ever wondered just how breathing works, you are already on your way to thinking like a scientist. In this book, we'll experiment with respiration. You can do these experiments with things you already have at home. You might need to catch your breath by the time we're finished!

Getting STARTED

Scientists learn by carefully studying how things and people work. For example, scientists who study humans watch how they develop. They see which parts of the body do what jobs and how each part is connected. They study the process of breathing and how the respiratory system works. They do experiments to see how the lungs use oxygen and **carbon dioxide** to keep the body healthy and working as it should.

Good scientists take notes on everything they discover. They record their **observations**. Sometimes those observations lead scientists to ask new questions. With new questions in mind, they design experiments to find the answers.

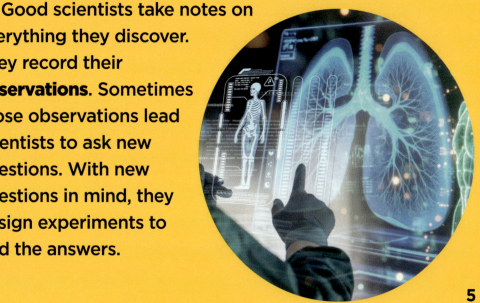

When scientists design experiments, they often use the scientific method. What is the scientific method? It's a step-by-step process to answer specific questions. The steps don't always follow the same pattern. However, the scientific method often works like this:

STEP ONE: A scientist gathers the facts and makes observations about one particular thing.

STEP TWO: The scientist comes up with a question that is not answered by observations and facts.

STEP THREE: The scientist creates a **hypothesis**. This is a statement about what the scientist thinks might be the answer to the question.

STEP FOUR: The scientist tests the hypothesis by designing an experiment to see whether the hypothesis is correct. Then the scientist carries out the experiment and writes down what happens.

STEP FIVE: The scientist draws a **conclusion** based on the result of the experiment. The conclusion might be that the hypothesis is correct. Sometimes, though, the hypothesis is not correct. In that case, the scientist might develop a new hypothesis and another experiment.

In the following experiments, we'll see the scientific method in action. We'll gather some facts and observations about respiration. And for each experiment, we'll develop a question and a hypothesis. Next, we'll do an actual experiment to see if our hypothesis is correct. By the end of the experiment, we should know something new about respiration. Scientists, are you ready? Then let's go!

EXPERIMENT 1

In Through the Nose...

Without any effort on your part, your body performs countless important jobs. It doesn't matter if you're studying for a test or taking a nap. Your heart keeps beating. Your eyes keep blinking. Your lungs keep breathing. It's a good thing, too. If any of these processes stopped, you would quickly be in big trouble.

Each day, you breathe about 20,000 times. Breathing, or respiration, starts with your mouth and nose. Most of the time, you breathe in through your nose. If you've ever had a cold with a stuffy nose, you know that you can also breathe through your mouth. When you exercise and need bigger quantities of oxygen, you tend to breathe through your mouth also.

Let's ask ourselves some interesting questions about breathing. For example, how do our nostrils work when we breathe? Do both of our nostrils breathe the same amount of air? Let's test this hypothesis: **The same amount of air passes through each nostril.**

Here's what you'll need:

- A small hand or pocket mirror
- Paper
- A pencil

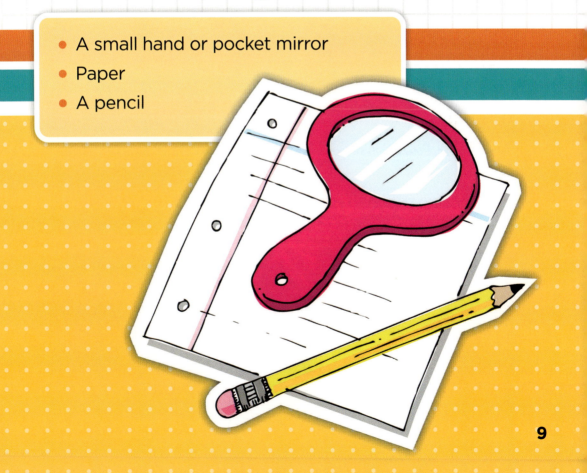

INSTRUCTIONS

1. First, exhale, or breathe out, through your nostrils onto your hand. Can you feel the warmth? As air travels through your body, it picks up heat.

2. Now hold the mirror up to your nose. Put it below your nose but above your upper lip. Keep it horizontal.

3. Breathe gently out of your nose onto the mirror.

4. Look at the mirror. Do you see **condensation**? It may look like fog clouding up the mirror. Record what you observe.

5. Look carefully. Can you see two spots, one from each nostril? The moisture from the breath of each nostril created condensation. Is one area of condensation bigger than the other? What does that suggest about the amount of air that passed through each nostril? Was your hypothesis correct?

CONCLUSION

Believe it or not, each nostril takes turns being the one through which most of your breath passes. Write down the time and which side seems to be doing the most work. Then wait 2 or 3 hours and repeat the experiment. You will likely see that most air now passes through the opposite nostril.

FACTS!

On March 27, 2021, freediver Budimir Šobat of Croatia set a new world record for holding his breath: 24 minutes and 37.36 seconds. How was this possible? It required years of practice and training. Šobat breathed rapidly with 100% pure oxygen for 30 minutes before his record-setting attempt. This raised the oxygen levels in his blood, which allowed him to hold his breath longer.

· EXPERIMENT 2 ·

Waste Gas and Cabbage Water

Breathing is all about inhaling and exhaling. We breathe in oxygen from the air. We need it for every cell in our bodies to grow and function. But after we use up the oxygen, we are left with a waste gas: carbon dioxide. Respiration involves exchanging these gases.

When you breathe in, what happens? First, the air passes through the **trachea**, or windpipe. This is the tube that connects your mouth and nose to your lungs. The trachea is about 4 inches (10.2 centimeters) long and less than 1 inch (2.5 cm) around. It is made up of

16–20 C-shaped pieces of strong, bendy tissue called **cartilage**. This cartilage keeps the trachea from collapsing.

The inside of your trachea is covered in tiny hair-like structures called cilia. As you breathe, they gently move back and forth, keeping mucus, dust, and dirt from entering your lungs.

You may be wondering how the carbon dioxide waste from this process leaves your body. Could it be through exhaling? Let's test this hypothesis: **When we breathe out, we exhale carbon dioxide.**

Here's what you'll need:

- An adult helper
- Red cabbage
- A sharp knife
- A pot (not aluminum)
- Water
- A strainer
- A clear glass
- A straw

INSTRUCTIONS

1. With an adult's help, chop up some red cabbage.

2. Put the cabbage into a pot and cover it with water.

3. Heat the cabbage on the stove until it begins to boil. It should keep boiling until the water turns purple.

4. Take the cabbage off the heat. Let the water and cabbage mixture cool.

5. Use the strainer to pour the juices from the pot into a clear glass. Do not fill the glass all the way to the top.

6. Put a straw in the glass and blow into it. Watch carefully.

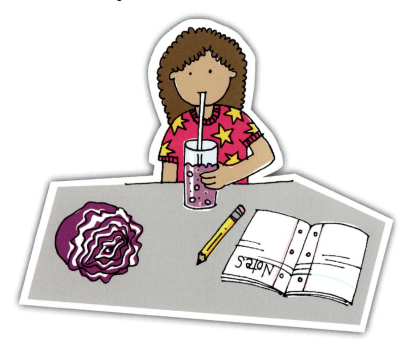

CONCLUSION

What happens to the color of the juice as you blow into the straw? Slowly, it will change from purple to pink. This is because red cabbage has a pigment called **anthocyanin**. Boiling the cabbage extracted this pigment, so the water was full of it. Fun fact: Anthocyanin turns pink or red when an acid is present. When you blew out through the straw, the carbon dioxide in your breath reacted with the water and turned into something called carbonic acid. So it turned the cabbage water pink! What does this fact tell you about the air you exhale? Does it contain carbon dioxide? Based on your observations, you can conclude that it does. Your hypothesis was correct!

EXPERIMENT 3

A Trip Through the Bronchi

At the bottom of your trachea are two large tubes. They are called the bronchi. One connects to the left lung, while the other connects to the right one. By itself, each tube is called a **bronchus**. Inside your lungs, the bronchi branch out like the limbs on a tree. As they spread out, they get smaller and smaller. The tiniest ones are about as thick as a strand of hair. These are called **bronchioles**. Each lung has about 30,000 of them!

At the end of each and every one of those tiny bronchioles are bunches of even tinier air sacs known as **alveoli**. You have about 600 million of them! Think of the alveoli as tiny bunches of grapes at the end of the bronchioles. As small as alveoli are, there are so many that if you could lay them out flat, they would cover a whole tennis court.

Can you guess what happens to your lungs when you inhale and air reaches all of these alveoli? Let's test a new hypothesis: **When alveoli fill up with air, the chest has to expand to make room.**

Here's what you'll need:

- A clear 16- to 20-ounce (about 1/2 liter) plastic bottle
- Water
- Food coloring
- A straw
- A small lump of clay

· INSTRUCTIONS ·

1. Start by filling the bottle halfway with water. Then add a few drops of food coloring.

2. Next, put the straw in the bottle and place the clay over the bottle's opening. This should hold the straw in place so it does not come out of the bottle. The straw is like your trachea, while the clay is like your throat. The bottle is your chest. The movement of the water represents the movement of air in and out of your lungs.

3. Now squeeze the bottle with your hand. This represents an exhale.

4. Watch what happens to the bottle. Do you see how it gets smaller? That's because the water has been pushed out. When you stop pushing on the bottle, it gets bigger. This is from air pressure pushing the water back in.

CONCLUSION

How did this experiment show you how your chest changes as you breathe in and out? Take a few extra breaths now. Can you picture the air sacs filling up and then emptying? That is what respiration is all about.

EXPERIMENT 4

How Much Air?

Lungs are some of the biggest organs in the body. They take up most of the room in your chest. The one on the left is slightly smaller than the one on the right because it has to make room for your heart. Because your heart and lungs are so vital to living, they are protected by 12 pairs of rib bones connected to your sternum, or breastbone.

When you imagine what your lungs are like, you may picture them as large, hollow bags or balloons that expand and contract. They are actually much more like pink, squishy sponges. As you've already learned, they're not empty either. They're full of bronchioles and alveoli.

How much air can a set of lungs hold? Do you think your body's size affects how much air your lungs can hold?

Here are three hypotheses to choose from:

Hypothesis #1: A smaller person's lungs hold less air than a larger person's lungs.

Hypothesis #2: A smaller person's lungs hold the same amount of air as a larger person's lungs.

Hypothesis #3: A smaller person's lungs hold more air than a larger person's lungs.

Here's what you'll need:

- A large dishpan or sink
- Water
- An empty 1-gallon (3.8-L) milk bottle with a lid
- A funnel
- 2 flexible drinking straws
- An adult helper

INSTRUCTIONS

1. Fill a dishpan or sink with 2 inches (5 cm) of water.

2. Fill the milk bottle all the way to the top with water. You may need to pour the water through the funnel to keep it from spilling. Put the lid on tightly. Most likely, a little water will squirt out when you do.

3. Now, holding the lid, turn the bottle upside down. Place the mouth of the bottle under the water in the dishpan.

4. Carefully reach under the water and unscrew the lid. Set the lid to the side.

5. Bend the straw and put the shorter end into the mouth of the bottle under the water. The longer end of the straw should stick up out of the water.

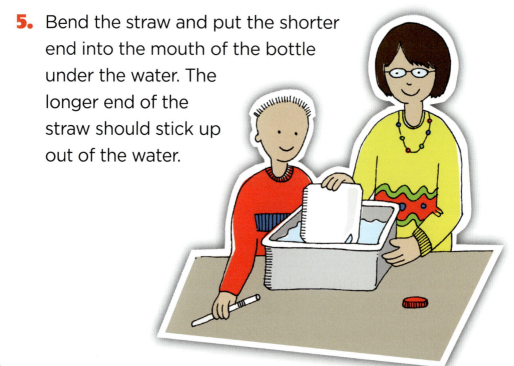

6. Have an adult hold the bottle while you hold the straw.

7. Pinch your nose closed and take a deep breath.

8. Blow all of your air into the straw in one strong breath. What happens to the water in the bottle?

9. Now reach in and put the lid back on the bottle tightly.

10. Remove the bottle from the dishpan. Set it on the table. How much water is in the bottle now?

11. Repeat the experiment. This time, have an adult blow into the second straw. What happens to the water in the bottle this time?

CONCLUSION

When you breathed into the straw, some water was forced out of the bottle. The amount of empty space you created in the bottle represents the amount of air that was in your lungs. How do your results compare to the adult's? Did the adult force more water out of the bottle? If so, why do you think that is? Most adults have bigger bodies than children. Their lungs are larger, too. And larger lungs can hold more air. Does this help explain your results? Was your hypothesis correct?

· EXPERIMENT 5 ·
It Takes Muscles

With all of the movement your lungs do, you might think that they have strong muscles. The surprise is that your lungs do not contain any muscles. Instead, a nearby muscle called the diaphragm plays a big role in helping them do their job.

The diaphragm is a dome-shaped muscle that curves up beneath your lungs. As you take a breath, the muscle flattens out and moves lower. This creates more space in your chest for your lungs, which get bigger when they fill with air. When the space in the chest is

increased, it lowers the pressure pushing in on the lungs. So, air moves into the lungs and they get bigger to fill the space. The muscles surrounding your ribs help, too. They lift the ribs up and out so your lungs can fill up.

What do you think happens to the diaphragm when you exhale? Here is a hypothesis: **As you exhale, the diaphragm relaxes and moves up.**

Here's what you'll need:

- Scissors
- 1 straw
- 2 small balloons
- 2 small rubber bands
- Rubber cement
- Tape
- 1 clear plastic cup
- 1 large balloon
- 1 large rubber band

INSTRUCTIONS

1. With the scissors, cut two 2-inch (5-cm) pieces from the straw. Cut a small triangle in the center of one of the 2-inch pieces. Do not cut through the opposite side of the straw.

2. Fit 1 small balloon over each end of the 2-inch pieces of straw, securing each balloon with a small rubber band.

3. Bend the straw outward in the middle of the triangular hole. If you need help, ask an adult.

4. Next, take the second 2-inch piece of straw. Cut a V shape at one end of the straw. Make sure you cut through both sides of the straw so that you have two slanted points at one end.

5. Fit the slanted points into the openings on each side of the bent straw. Using the rubber cement, glue the two pieces of the straw together. Put tape over the seal you made with the rubber cement, and give it at least 30 minutes to dry.

6. While it is drying, cut a hole the same width as the straw in the bottom of the clear plastic cup. From the inside of the cup, push the straight 2-inch piece of straw

through the hole in the cup. The small balloons and the straw they are attached to should now be inside the plastic cup. Use the rubber cement to glue the straight 2-inch piece of straw in place.

7. Next, take the large balloon and cut the neck off of it. Stretch it carefully over the opening of the cup. Don't crack the cup. Secure the edges with the large rubber band.

8. Pull down on the large balloon gently. Observe what happens to the small balloons. Let go of the large balloon. What happens to the small balloons now?

CONCLUSION

The large balloon represents your diaphragm. Pulling the large balloon recreates what happens when you inhale. When you pulled the balloon, you created more space in the cup and the pressure on the small balloons decreased. So air entered them. What happened when you released the large balloon? Did it move back into its original position? What happened to the smaller lung balloons? Releasing the large balloon recreates what happens when you exhale. Your diaphragm and rib muscles have relaxed. With less space in the chest, the pressure increases. The air is forced out of your lungs. Did you prove your hypothesis?

· EXPERIMENT 6 ·

Do It Yourself!

Now you know many things about your respiratory system. You learned through your observations and experiments. You even created hypotheses and tested them! So what's next?

How about coming up with your own experiment? First, you need to think of a question that you would like to answer. For example, have you ever wondered how many breaths you take in a minute? Do you think different activities might change the number of breaths? What kinds of activities might affect your breathing the most? Come up with answers to these questions. Then test them!

Think about the materials you will need to do this experiment. Write out a list of these materials. Then write out the instructions for your experiment. Work with a friend, a classmate, or a family member to perform your experiment. Make sure to record your results. Congratulations! You're now a full-fledged junior scientist.

Glossary

alveoli (al-VEE-uh-liye) tiny air-filled sacs in the lungs

anthocyanin (an-thuh-SAHY-uh-nuhn) a pigment that produces blue and red coloring in plants

bronchioles (BRONG-kee-ohlz) tiny extensions of the bronchi

bronchus (BRONG-kuhs) one branch of the trachea

carbon dioxide (KAHR-buhn diye-AHK-siyed) a gas that is a mixture of carbon and oxygen

cartilage (KAHR-tuh-lij) an elastic type of connective tissue

conclusion (kuhn-KLOO-zhuhn) a final decision, thought, or opinion

condensation (kahn-den-SAY-shuhn) the process of changing from a gas to a liquid

hypothesis (hahy-POTH-uh-sis) a logical guess about what will happen in an experiment

observations (ahb-suhr-VAY-shuhnz) things that are seen or noticed with one's senses

respiration (reh-spuh-RAY-shuhn) the inhalation and exhalation of air

trachea (TRAY-kee-uh) the windpipe that connects the mouth to the lungs

For More Information

BOOKS

Crane, Cody. *Respiratory System.* A True Book: Your Amazing Body. Danbury, CT: Children's Press, 2024.

Midthun, Joseph. Samuel Hiti (illustrator). *The Respiratory System.* Building Blocks of the Human Body. Chicago: World Book, Ann Arbor, MI: Cherry Lake Publishing, 2022.

Human Body: Lungs and Respiratory System. Knowledge Encyclopedia for Children. Delhi, India: Wonder House Books, 2023.

WEBSITES
Explore these online sources with an adult:

Biology | Secret of our Respiratory System (PART 1) | How Do the Lungs Work? | Science for Kids | YouTube

Lungs and Respiratory System | TeensHealth

The Respiratory System for Kids video | Learn Bright | YouTube

Index

alveoli, 16–17, 20
alveoli experiment, 16–19

bronchi, 16
bronchioles, 16, 20

cabbage experiment, 12–15
carbon dioxide, 5, 12–13
carbon dioxide experiment, 12–15
cartilage, 13
chest expansion experiments, 16–19, 24–27
cilia, 13
conclusions, 6, 11, 15, 19, 23, 27

diaphragm, 24–25, 27
diaphragm experiment, 24–27
do-it-yourself experiment, 28–29

exhalation experiments, 12–15, 24–27

heart, 8, 20
hypotheses, 6–7, 9–10, 13, 15, 17, 21, 23, 25, 27

lungs, 5, 8, 12–13, 16–18, 20–21, 23–25, 27
lung size experiment, 20–23

muscles, 24–25, 27

nose, 8, 10, 12, 23
nostrils, 9–11
nostrils experiment, 8–11
notes, 5

observations, 5–7, 15, 28
oxygen, 5, 9, 11–12

scientific method, 6–7
scientists, 4–7, 29
sternum, 20

trachea, 12–13, 16, 18

world record, 11

About the Author

Tamra B. Orr is the author of more than 500 nonfiction books for readers of all ages. She loves doing research. Orr lives in the Pacific Northwest. She and her husband have four children. She has a teaching degree from Ball State University and in her few minutes of spare time, she likes to write old-fashioned letters, read books, and look at the snowcapped mountains.